SHORTSTOP SUPREME

Dominating the Diamond

The Shortstop's Bible

Skills, Drills, and Thrills

SKY BENSON

Table of Contents

CHAPTER 1

THE SHORTSTOP STANCE

Fielding fundamentals

"And footwork."

There is a good reason why the shortstop position is frequently referred to as the "heart and soul" of the infield offense. They are the defensive linemen entrusted with turning sharply hit balls into outs. They are the ones who patrol the broad middle area. When it comes to mastering this stance, however, it is not enough to possess a powerful arm or daring dive. The fundamentals of fielding and footwork are the building blocks upon which a superb shortstop foundation is built. When it comes to clean plays, quick throws, and ultimately, outs on the board, these seemingly simple qualities form the foundation that holds everything together.

The Crucial Position

To become a fielding genius, the first thing you need to do is build a comfortable and practical stance. Create an image of oneself as a coiled spring, ready to react instantly. "Shoulder-width apart, knees slightly bent," the feet should be positioned. When in this position, it is possible to do rapid bursts in any direction. Having a low center of gravity is beneficial for maintaining stability and balance. Consider the situation of an athlete about to participate in a competition. The glove should be held at chest height, and the fingers should be relaxed but ready to contract around the ball. The second hand must be comfortably positioned outside the glove, prepared to aid in catching. The eyes look around the entire field, focusing on the hitter and the pitcher. Looking forward is essential!

The silent symphony that begins with footwork

It's time to get those feet going, shall we? Footwork executed correctly is comparable to a quiet symphony, a coordinated dance that results in effortless plays. When approaching a ground ball, you should avoid chasing it immediately before you get close to it. To get in front of the ball, you should instead shuffle laterally while taking short, rapid strides (think of them as "chop steps"). Because of this, you can maintain control and respond appropriately to any change in the direction. As you approach the ball, plant your lead foot (typically your right foot for right-handed throwers) and extend your glove hand to field the ball. This is the fielding technique. To maintain stability, keep your body low and centered. The first step in the throwing process is to transfer the ball to your throwing hand and then pivot your body toward the target after successfully catching the ball. In this moment, the enchantment of footwork comes into play. To gain momentum for the throw, many shortstops employ a shuffle stride with the foot opposite their right foot (in this case, their left foot). Because of this, the transition from fielding to throwing is made more seamless.

Getting Familiar with the Various Types of Balls

Some ground balls are superior to others. When you receive a ball hit to your backhand side, you should take a crossover step with your opposite foot (the left foot for right-handed throwers) to place your body comfortably to field the ball. The phrase "on the run": If you hit a shot deep in the hole, your first concentration should be catching the ball. You may need to modify your throwing action to accommodate your momentum; nonetheless, a clean catch is always the most important thing. Line drives demand minimum footwork and quick reflexes to be an effective technique. Maintain a low stance and concentrate on grabbing the ball with your glove as you perform your stance. If the circumstances warrant it, you might be required to make a hasty exit.

Practice makes perfect

Let's put the theory into practice now that you have a comprehensive understanding of it. Cone drills involve arranging cones in a square configuration and practicing shuffling laterally around them to simulate fielding movements. The Ground Ball Machine is an excellent piece of equipment that allows you to practice fielding various ground balls that come from some directions and run at varying speeds. You should grab a squad member and ask them to throw you ground balls from multiple angles. Practicing your response time and hand-eye coordination in this manner is an excellent improvement method! This drill is designed to imitate the rapid-fire action of turning a double play. Your second baseman should be working with you to improve your footwork, throwing, and communication skills. Repetition is essential, so keep that in mind. When you try to perform these drills, you will find that perfect footwork becomes more familiar. In a short time, you can respond immediately, making those problematic plays appear effortless.

Outside of the realm of mechanics, the mental edge

Although mechanics are essential, a great shortstop has a highly developed mental game. Read the batter and the scenario before you make your move. Observe the pitcher's delivery and the hitter's swing to determine where the ball will travel. Communicate with your teammates (also known as "communication")! Make a precise and unambiguous request for the ball to avoid any confusion. To have confidence, you must have faith in yourself! Even though mistakes are inevitable, a self-assured shortstop has a greater chance of recovering and making the next play.

You can progress by understanding these principles,
Footwork and mental components.

Handling ground balls

"And line drives."

The middle ground is yours as a shortstop. You rule the infield like a king or queen and love hitting ground balls and line drives. But getting good at these plays that look easy takes a mix of skill, timing, and quick reflexes. Here is the complete guide to handling line drives and ground balls like a pro:

Basics of Ground Ball

The most common type of hit ball is a ground ball. Don't go after the ball straight on. Instead, move side to side in small, quick "chop steps" toward the direction the ball is expected to take. This steady action helps you keep your balance and adapt to changes in direction. The best way to go to the field relies on the sport. When facing a pull player (someone who hits their power side), move a little deeper to prepare for a hard-hit ground ball. If you're facing a slap hitter, on the other hand, you should play deeper to stop any possible infield dribblers. Put your glove hand out low and toward the ground. Keep your fingers loose but get ready to close around the ball. Keep your other hand out of the glove and be prepared to help if someone needs it. When you touch the ball, move it smoothly to your throwing hand. This transfer should go quickly and smoothly, with as little moving as possible. Once you've moved the ball, start the throw by turning your body toward the goal, which is usually first base. For strength, use your lower body, and for accuracy, follow through with your throwing arm.

How to Control the Line Drive

Line drives happen faster and in different ways than ground balls. For line drives, do as little walking as possible. Keep your stance low and work on your hand-eye balance to quickly grab the ball with your glove. Play a little deeper than usual for line drives, especially if runners are on base. This extra room allows you to react and catch the ball without diving. Do drills that feel like line drives to improve your reactions. You can work on catching fast-moving balls with a buddy or a hitting machine. Not every line drive is the same. A diving catch is sometimes crucial, but safety should always come first. A controlled jump or a backpedal might be better if you can't get to the ball with your feet.

Getting Good at Different Ground Balls

Not every ground ball is easy to hit. For backhand plays, you need to make a small change to your technique. Do a lateral step with the foot that is not your dominant to set up your body to catch the ball backhanded. Focus on a smooth change to your throwing hand as you keep your glove low. When the ball is deep, seeing it is the most important thing. Change how you throw based on your speed, but get out before making a solid throw. Bunts need quick responses and an eye on the ball. You should charge and field the ball like any other ground ball, but be ready to throw to a different base if necessary.

Drills to Master Ground Ball and Line Drive

This is a great tool that lets you practice catching ground balls that come at you from different directions and at different speeds. Play "Partner Toss" with a teammate. Have them throw you ground balls and line drives from various positions. You can improve your reaction time and hand-eye balance by doing this. Place cones in a square shape and practice moving around them like you're catching a ground ball. To make line shots, use tennis balls or other light balls. Have a buddy throw the balls randomly in different directions so you must react quickly and catch them. Work on making double plays with your second baseman. Footwork, throwing, talking to each other, and being able to handle ground balls well are all part of this drill.

The mental edge you need for fielding

Read the player and the situation to get ready. You can guess where the ball will go by watching how the thrower throws and how the batter swings. You can then set yourself up for the best chance of getting out. Talk to your friends! Call for the ball clearly and firmly to avoid misunderstanding, especially during close plays. Keep your faith in yourself! Slip-ups: If the shortstop is sure of themselves, they are likelier to make the next play after making a mistake. Don't think about mistakes too much. Quickly look at what went wrong, then move on to the next play. Having a bad attitude will only get in the way of your work. Say positive things to yourself to boost your mood. Phrases like "Next play" or "I got this" can help you stay on track and keep you going. Don't be afraid to learn from your mistakes. Look at replays or discuss them with your teacher to determine what you can do better.

You do a lot of ground balls and line drives. If you can master these, you'll be the best player on the field. You can go from being an excellent shortstop to a fielding machine ready to make any ball an out if you put in the time and effort to practice, work on your mental game, and keep improving your skill. Now go play in the middle and show everyone why they call you the "Shortstop Supreme"!

Developing a quick

"And accurate throw"

Your arm is your tool as a shortstop. It's what turns hard-hit balls into outs and makes those exciting double plays possible. But having a strong arm isn't enough. To take over the middle ground, you need to be able to throw quickly and accurately. Here are some steps you can take to make throws that make base runners scared:

The Way a Strong Throw Works

The proper mechanics are the first step to a good throw. "The Grip" means to hold the ball easily across the seams with your fingers spread out. A good grip gives you control and gives the ball a spin to get it right. The windup provides the throw with its speed. To begin, spread your feet shoulder-width apart and curl up a bit. Bring back for more strength and raise the glove with the ball to your ear. Take a decisive step toward the goal with your other foot (left foot for right-handed throwers). This gives your arm motion and moves power from your lower body to your arm. As you reward, quickly turn your hips toward the target. In turn, this gives the throw a lot of power. Point your elbow high and toward the receiver as your pitching arm toward the catcher.

This ensures the ball is released smoothly and at the right speed. Don't stop once you throw the ball away. Move your whole body toward the target for the most power and efficiency. At the end, point your front foot at the goal.

Getting good at the throwing transfer

A vital part of a quick throw is moving from the glove to the throwing hand. When you catch the ball, bring your throwing hand toward your glove to meet the ball in the air. This gets rid of moving and delays that aren't needed. Squeeze the glove a little as you move the ball to make a firm grip and start moving it toward your throwing hand. Keep the ball firmly in your throwing hand as you finish the move. When you throw, a loose grip can make you miss.

Getting better at throwing

If your arm is strong, you can throw the ball faster and get more outs. In this famous drill, you throw the ball farther and farther over time. Start at a comfortable distance and slowly move it farther away as your arm strength improves. Add weighted balls to your practice for throwing. Because these balls add force, your arm muscles must work harder, making you more robust in the long run. Begin with smaller weights and work your way up to heavier ones. Good form is significant to stay healthy. Your lower body gets stronger through exercises like jump squats and box jumps. This gives you more power when you throw.

Improving the accuracy of your throws

A strong arm is useless if you can't aim with great accuracy. Setting targets at different distances and practicing throwing strikes reliably is called "target practice." You can get a feel for the distance and path of your throws this way. Have a partner throw you ground balls and line drives from different angles. Make sure you can throw accurately and quickly to each base. For accuracy, you need to have good movement when you throw. Focusing on balance, timing, and where to put your feet during drills can help you throw more consistently.

Getting faster at throwing

Even though the aim is still fundamental, being able to throw faster can help you. If you work on your throwing mechanics, you can throw faster. Pay attention to how well you move strength from your legs to your arms. During the throw, explosive hip movement creates a lot of power—strengthen your core muscles to get the most out of this movement. A small wrist snap can give your throws more zip when you let go. However, control should come before too much wrist movement.

Mental toughness is essential for throwing well.

Your mind is a vital part of throwing well. Picture yourself effectively throwing things with perfect form. This practice can boost your confidence and efficiency. Don't let runners or the stress of the situation distract you. Pay close attention to your goal and how to throw the ball. Getting jitters in high-pressure scenarios can make it harder to throw accurately. To keep your cool, use relaxation methods like deep breathing.

Drills to bring out your best throwing machine

In this drill, you and a partner throw the ball back and forth as fast as possible. This helps you throw faster and coordinate your hands and eyes better. Hitting fungo grounders to yourself pushes you to the field and throws quickly, like being in a fast-paced game. You can work on your footwork and follow through without a partner when you throw against a wall. It can be helpful to throw weighted balls, but make sure you use the proper form and slowly add more weight to keep from hurting yourself.

Getting good at throwing quickly and accurately takes time and hard work. Be patient, keep practicing, and work on getting better at your skills. Don't give up when things go wrong; learn from them and keep trying to improve. If you work hard and do things correctly, you can turn your throws into a tool that makes base runners and other teams afraid! Now get outside and let your inner throwing machine loose!

14

CHAPTER 2

Mastering the Double Play

Techniques

"For turning two smoothly."

The two-for-one. It's a beautiful sight in baseball to see players think quickly, move together, and throw the ball precisely. You're the most important player on defense as a shortstop. It's not as easy as it looks to turn two quickly, though. It takes a lot of practice, good conversation, and knowledge of the rules before the game. Here's everything you need to know to become a double-play master:

Getting ready is vital.

It's essential to get along well with your second baseman. Talk about the different double plays that could happen and agree on the throwing angles and signs for communication. Look at the players on the other team. Knowing their habits (like whether they pull, hit, or slap) can help you guess where the ground ball will go and where to stand during the game.

Read the situation

Watch how the pitcher throws and how the batter swings. For a faster response time, this lets you guess where the ball will be hit and move yourself accordingly. For example, "Calling the Ball" means that information must be clear. Being the shortstop implies that calling for the ball is your job. Say "Short!" or "Two!" in a clear voice to let the second baseman know if you or he will take the out at first.

Perfect Stepping

Don't go after the ball straight on. To get to the ball, stay on your toes and move side to side with quick steps. This lets you cleanly catch the ball and respond quickly to the throw. When you field the ball, see it with a smooth glove movement and focus on rapidly moving your throwing hand to the ball. Start the throw to second base with a decisive turn. Use your lower body for strength and throw quickly and accurately.

The Art of the Pivot

The pivot is a vital part of turning two. Place your back foot firmly on the ground and turn your front foot toward second base. Picture putting your front foot across the ball. "The Glove Transfer" means to move the ball smoothly from your glove to your throwing hand as you turn. This cuts down on wasted time and action. Turn your upper body toward the second base to get more power for the throw.

Synergy with the Second Base

The second baseman needs to "break" toward the first base after getting the ball from you. This slows down the runner and makes the throwing lane faster for the team to throw to first. Setting up visual or audible cues will help the second baseman know whether to play the ball deep or shallow, based on the situation (for example, a deep ground ball vs. a sharply hit ball).

Getting Good at Different Double Play Situations

Every double-play is not the same. If the out at second base is a force-out, you should focus on making a quick throw to the second baseman. After that, the first baseman can take their time getting the out at first. Catching the ball is the most important thing when it is hit deep. If you want to throw quickly to second base, even if it's imperfect, change how you throw. When there is a runner on third, you should throw home to get out first. This is called a "double play." But don't throw without looking; make sure there is a clear path to the catcher.

Drills for double-team dominance

The most critical drill you need to do. You and your second baseman should practice different double plays. Work on your timing, communication, and movement. This tool lets you work on catching ground balls and starting double plays at various speeds and angles. Get a teammate to throw you ground balls meant to be seen in double plays. Pay attention to communication signs, quick transfers, and throws to second.

How to Think Like a Double Play Winner

Stay focused on the play the whole time. It's important not to let other things confuse you. For a double play to work, you must be able to talk to your partners. You speak confidently and confidently to avoid uncertainty, especially on close plays. Double plays often happen when things get tough. Use relaxation techniques like deep breathing to stay calm and make quick choices. Mess-ups happen to even the best shortstops. After the game, look at what you did wrong and improve. Talk about replays with your teacher or teammates to determine how to improve your technique.

It takes a lot of hard work, practice, and teamwork to turn two quickly. You can become a double-play maestro by developing skills, communication, and mental game skills. This will make the other team afraid. Now, go out there and work with your friends to get out of those double plays.

Building chemistry

"With your second baseman"

In the middle infield, there is a beautiful dance of waiting, talking, and doing everything perfectly. As a shortstop, the second baseman is your partner in this complicated dance. A strong connection with them is the key to a good infield defense, which can turn impossible plays into easy outs. Instructions for getting along with your second baseman so that you can both be great at defense:

Communication: The Key to Making Connections

An excellent middle infield pair needs to be able to talk to each other constantly. Talk to your second baseman about what could happen before the game. You should talk about how you'll handle different kinds of ground balls, double plays, and other situations. As the shortstop, it's your job to call for the ball most of the time. To avoid misunderstanding, use precise words like "Short!" or "Two!" Use scheduled visual cues during your calls, such as a head nod or a hand signal, to improve conversation and help people act naturally. They keep talking to each other during the whole game. Talk about possible double plays based on the batter and men on base. Create an atmosphere where you feel comfortable talking about problems or offering changes during the game.

Drills to Improve Your Communication

"Double Play Turns" is the most essential part of conversation drills. Focus on clear calls, throws, and preparation as you practice different double plays. Get a partner and have them throw you ground balls from various directions. Learn how to call for the ball, throw it, and talk to your partner like in a game. Set up different hand signs or body language cues for various situations, like "deep ground ball" or "runner on third." Work on these signs together until you can do them without thinking.

Beyond Words: How to Read Body Language

It's not just words that send a message. Watch where your partner stands before the pitch to see how they place their body. This can help you figure out where to stand and show you how they think the ball will go. Look at how they're putting on their gloves. If they raise their hand, it could mean they're ready to throw, and if they lower it, it could mean they want the ball. Look your partner in the eyes for a short time before the pitch. This can help you understand each other's goals even better.

Making Friends and Trust

Show respect for each other's choices and skills. If you don't agree with someone on a call, say so in a relaxed and helpful way. Help and encourage each other. Everyone makes mistakes. A pat on the back or a nice word after a good play can boost morale and confidence. Look at your mistakes together and use them to learn how to talk to each other and work together better.

Creating an Environment That Is Fun and Helpful

If you want to make your dream come true, remember that you are part of a team. As a team, celebrate your wins and work through problems. Keep a positive mood on the field. Making jokes and having good conversations can help you relax and talk to others better. Taking part in team events outside of practice can help you get to know your second baseman better and build relationships with other players on the team.

How to Work Together Easily on Game Day

Do double plays and talking drills during warm-ups to ensure everyone is on the same page before the game starts. Change how you talk to people during the game depending on what's happening. For instance, you might use more spoken cues when the batter is slow, but quick visual cues might work better when the batter is fast. After each inning, talk briefly about any communication problems. Find things you can do better and change how you do things for the next game.

How to Learn from the Pros

Watch skilled middle infielders who are known for getting along with each other. You can find methods you can use in your game by observing how they talk and hold themselves. Your trainers may be able to help you. Talk to them about ways to communicate and get feedback on how you're working together with your second baseman.

It takes time and effort to get along with your second baseman. It's an ongoing process that needs steady work from both of you. You can make your middle infield into an impenetrable wall by prioritizing clear communication, practicing together, building trust and respect, and keeping a positive mood. This will make rival batters frustrated and leave base runners stranded.

Quick transfers

"And avoiding base runner interference."

As a shortstop, you're the conductor of the middle infield, putting together plays with lightning-fast throws and smooth catching. But there is an essential step between catching the ball and throwing it like a laser: switching from glove to throwing hand. This simple action can make or break a play, especially when fast runners are on base, and the possibility of an interference call is always there. Here is the best way to learn how to make quick moves and keep the game moving smoothly:

This is how a quick transfer works.

Keeping your glove tight but not stiff as you catch the ball is essential. Switching to your throwing hand is easy when your grip is relaxed but solid. Bring your throwing hand toward the glove at the same time that you catch the ball. This cuts down on stretching that isn't necessary and speeds up the transfer point. Move the ball into the pocket of your throwing hand with your fingertips. If you touch the ball, it takes longer to get to the other player. Hold the ball tightly with your fingers spread across the edges once you have the ball in your throwing hand. This gives you control for a good throw.

Better with practice: drills for quick glove work

To begin, work on one-handed moves against a wall. Always throw the ball from your glove to your throwing hand, ensuring the move is smooth and quick. Grab a partner and ask them to throw you ground balls from different directions. Ensure you catch the ball properly with your glove and quickly switch to your throwing hand before you throw to a target. For quick response drills, use tennis balls or other light balls. Have a buddy throw the balls all over the place to make it look like ground balls are being hit at different speeds and spins. Get better at quickly catching and moving the ball.

Advanced Transfer Methods for a Wide Range of Situations

Not every ground ball is the same. Before you play with your backhand, cross your other foot over the other foot to get your body in a good position. Focus on a smooth transition to your throwing hand, even if it's a little backhanded. Keep your glove low. When the ball is deep, catching it is the most important thing. Focus on making the catch as you get close to the ball, then make a quick transfer while keeping your speed in check before throwing. Speed is critical in double plays. As quickly as possible, make the move while keeping the ball in your hands. Aim for a clean transfer point so your throw to second base doesn't take too long.

How to Keep Base Runners from Interfering

It's a careful balance to make plays at shortstop while staying out of the way of runners on base. Learn the actual rules about what happens when a base runner gets in the way of another runner.

Knowing the rules' limits will help you plan your moves to avoid breaking them. Keep an eye on the baserunners the whole time the play is going on. Keep an eye on their movements and guess where they'll go to escape running into them. A clean catch means you don't have to make as many offensive plays around the runner. Pay attention to how easily you field the ball, so you have more time and space to make a legal throw. Keep your body under control while you play. Stay away from lunging or making violent moves that could hit the runner. Tell the runner on first base that you will catch the ball by speaking or moving your body. This can help them change their path so they don't run into anything.

Practice Makes Perfect: Drills to Stay Out of the Way

Use live baserunners during practice scrimmages to make them more like real games. Pay attention to fielding the ball neatly and staying in the right place to avoid contact. While you work on fielding ground balls, have a partner run base running drills. This lets you guess how the runner will move and change your position accordingly. Check out close plays where interference was called. Look at how you're standing and moving your body to find ways to improve.

The mental edge

"Focus on the Ball" means to keep your full attention on the ball the whole time. Don't let runners on base or other things distract you. Guess where the ball will go and how fast it will go. This enables you to set up your throwing hand beforehand, so the shift goes more smoothly. Have faith that you can make the play. When you have confidence, you can respond and move more quickly and smoothly. Improve your ability to make quick decisions. Quickly look at the situation and decide the best play, with a legal catch and throw coming first.

How to Stay Sharp During the Game

Warm-Up Before the Game: Do transfer drills to prepare your hands and mind for smooth glove work. Pay attention to each play throughout the game. Don't get comfortable because of a past mistake or a regular ground ball. Before each pitch, picture a play that goes well. Picture yourself getting a clean catch on the ball, moving quickly, and throwing it like a rocket. Visualizing good things can make you feel better about yourself and help you respond faster.

Why footwork is important

Learn different footwork patterns for each case, such as backhand and on-the-run plays. This makes it easier to place the body and move it around. Stay balanced during the whole game. This gives you more control over your body and allows you to act quickly when something unexpected arises. As part of your training, do agility drills to improve your footwork and general defensive movement.

How to Learn from the Experts

Look at professional shortstops who are known for moving the ball quickly. Look at how they set up their bodies and hands to make movements go swiftly and smoothly. Your teachers may be the most helpful people you have. Ask them to look at how you transfer and tell you what you could do better.

It takes time, hard work, and a mix of mental and physical skills to get good at quick moves and avoiding interference. You'll become a defensive wizard if you regularly do drills, stay focused during games, and learn the rules well. Base runners will be afraid to challenge you, and your throws will go straight to the target, making the other team mad and bringing your team one step closer to success. Now, get out there and work on your skills. Make quick passes your signature move on the field.

CHAPTER 3

RANGE AND REFLEXES

Exercises to increase

"Lateral movement"

The agility and quickness that you possess are your tools as a shortstop. You need lightning-fast reactions when playing baseball, such as anticipating grounders, cutting off throws, and turning double plays into outs. Despite this, agility is not solely about speed in a straight path. To dominate the middle infield, it is essential to have a strong command of lateral movement, which involves moving from side to side with explosive power. A comprehensive guide of exercises that will help you become a master of lateral movement is included below for your convenience:

When it comes to lateral movement

When you engage in lateral movement, you move your body from side to side in short bursts. When you react to ground balls, you should quickly shift course to field balls that have been hit with a sharp hit. You should intercept throws from outfielders coming in at different angles when you cut off throws. To execute double plays, you must quickly advance toward the second base to receive throws and then relay them to the first base.

Putting the Foundation Together: Strength and Stability Incorporating

It is essential to ensure you have a solid foundation before beginning more challenging drills. You might think of your core as the dynamo that drives your movements. Exercises such as planks, side planks, and Russian twists are recommended to increase core stability and make it possible to perform explosive lateral movements. Having strong legs is necessary to generate power. Squats, lunges, and step-ups will strengthen your quadriceps, hamstrings, and glutes, giving you the required explosive push for swift lateral shifts.

The arsenal of drills that focus on laterally moving the body

This foundational drill is an absolute necessity to perform. First, position your feet shoulder-width apart and maintain a low center of gravity. Then, shuffle from side to side while taking short, fast steps. The speed should be gradually increased, and high knees should be incorporated for an additional challenge. These are similar to lunges, except instead of moving forward, you move them laterally. After lowering your hips and stepping out to the side with one leg, you should push yourself back to the starting position. Perform alternating leg movements while concentrating on keeping your center of gravity low. Cones should be arranged in a star configuration. To maximize the time spent touching each cone, begin in the middle and move laterally through the cones. Because of this, your footwork and agility will be tested in various directions. Explode side-to-side while landing softly on each foot. This is the lateral movement. Maximize the distance you jump and reduce the amount of time that passes between each jump.

In a line, place cones at a distance of ten to fifteen yards apart. After you have reached the first cone and touched it, you should race back to the starting location. Continue as you run to the second cone, back, etc. Both lateral movement and endurance are improved as a result of this.

Enhancing the Performance of Lateral Movement Drills: Taking It to the Next Level

Arrange cones in a square configuration according to your preference. Move laterally to each cone, picking up a ball placed there and then throwing it to a target before moving on to the next cone. Consequently, this integrates lateral movement with the mechanics of pitching. It is possible to perform lateral box jumps by jumping laterally onto a box, landing gently, and then quickly jumping back down it. With this, your explosive power and coordination will be tested.

The agility ladder can be used with a ball. In addition to performing drills on the agility ladder that involve lateral movement, you should also throw a ball against a wall or to a partner. Additionally, footwork, hand-eye coordination, and throwing mechanics are all incorporated into this.

The Crucial Role of Progress

Instead of trying to accomplish too much too quickly, you should begin slowly and gradually increase the intensity of your workout. While you are getting more robust and more comfortable, you should start with modest, controlled movements and progressively increase the speed and intricacy of your movements. Putting perfect form ahead of speed is the most important thing to remember to ensure you acquire healthy movement patterns; this will help you avoid injuries. Take rest days when required, and do not force yourself to continue working despite pain.

Tips for dominating the field

Getting Warmed Up Before engaging in any baseball activity, you should always do dynamic stretches and light lateral movement drills. This will help you prepare your muscles and enhance your range of motion. Maintaining a positive mental game is of the utmost importance. Maintain your concentration on the play, try to guess where the ball will go, and picture yourself responding swiftly and effectively throughout the game. Exercises that include lateral movement should not be contained entirely inside your training regimen. It is essential to incorporate them into your practice sessions so that you can establish muscle memory and simulate game circumstances. Maintaining focus on each play throughout the game is necessary for success on game day. Avoid allowing distractions or a mistake you made in the past to prevent you from concentrating. To ensure success, you should picture yourself doing a fluid play with swift lateral movement before each pitch. Visualization of favorable outcomes can help you feel more confident and improve your reaction time.

The Benefits That Extend Beyond the Realm

Exercises that focus on lateral movement are not limited to baseball. Improving Your Overall Fitness Lateral movement workouts improve your agility, coordination, and balance, improving your overall fitness and lowering the likelihood of sustaining an injury. These drills will help you improve your reflexes, allowing you to react quickly in various scenarios.

Improvements in Confidence: Mastering lateral movement on the field will increase your confidence in your overall movement capabilities.

Incorporating these workouts and advice into your routine will allow you to transform yourself into a machine capable of doing lateral movements. You will emerge victorious with lightning-fast reactions to the ground ball's effortless ability to cut off throws and turn double plays like a seasoned veteran. Maintaining consistency is essential. Commit some of your time to these activities, push yourself, and watch as your agility improves before your very eyes. Assist your team in securing victories by dominating the middle infield, leaving opposing batters disappointed, and ensuring that your team will win!

Anticipating hits

"And improving reaction time."

If you are a shortstop, you are the director of the symphony that plays in the infield while you are playing. On the other hand, to lead dazzling plays, you must first be able to anticipate the music. This implies that you must be able to anticipate where the ball will travel when it is hit off the bat. This article will teach you how to enhance your capacity to predict events and how to turn your response time into a defensive defense. Both of these skills will be covered in this post.

In the realm of art, the significance of anticipation

The sensation of anticipation is not merely a hunch but the cumulative effect of many factors. To learn how to read the pitcher, you must first watch how they throw the ball. Pay attention to their windup, the angle of their arms, and where the ball is located. Most of the time, pitchers who have a great deal of expertise will telegraph their pitches. For instance, a fastball can have a different windup than a curveball. Research the hitters on the opposing team using the information provided in the scouting reports. You can feel where they could try to hit the ball if you know their patterns, such as whether they are a pull hitter or a slapper. This is doable if you are aware of all of their patterns. The stance and body language of the hitter: It is essential to pay attention to the target's body language and particular stance. They appear crouching in a low position, ready for a fastball to contact them. Would it look like they are leaning back, possibly in preparation for a pitch that will change the direction of the pitch?

Putting Observation into Action: The Process of What Happens Next

Adjust the placement of your pre-pitch pitch per your anticipation by using the information you are anticipating getting a ground ball to your right; the most effective method to prevent yourself from losing your balance is to go slightly to the right side of the diamond. If you want to improve the speed with which you take your first step, you should focus on taking a quick first step in the direction you believe the ball will go. This information gives you an advantage when responding to the attack's location.

What Are the Implications of Working to Improve Your Reaction Time?

While working out, you could practice your response time by collecting tennis balls thrown from various places. This will help you improve your reaction time. As a result of engaging in these activities, your brain and body will be trained to react quickly to unexpected inputs. The mirror drills are below: You should work with another player and give them instructions to emulate the actions of the pitcher who is pitching. To improve your footwork and first-step quickness, you can practice reacting to their motions as if it were a genuine pitch. This will help you improve your footwork. Having the ability to "visualize having success"

Before each pitch, you should try to visualize yourself making a clean play and reacting quickly to the ball. Visualizing yourself in a good light can assist you in feeling more confident and will improve your ability to respond quickly.

It is true that to become flawless, one must practice tactics for the field.

You need to maintain your focus on each pitch throughout the game. A mistake you committed in the past or other distractions should not be allowed to hinder you from concentrating on what you are doing. It is essential to communicate with your partner. Depending on your observations, speak with your second baseman about how the ground ball could go. Always be on the lookout for future adjustments: You mustn't let the pitcher's delivery method fool you. If the pitch differs from what you had anticipated, you should be prepared to adjust your expectations accordingly.

A Psychological Advantage

Having a strong mental game is quite significant in terms of response time. If you want to be successful in the game, you should have confidence in your ability to make decisions. Develop the capacity to rely on your instincts and the facts you see to make wise decisions. A strategy for maintaining composure in high-pressure situations: It is impossible to avoid encounters with sources of pressure. Paying attention to your breathing and mentally clear your thoughts is essential to respond calmly and effectively.

To enhance your ability to predict and respond to circumstances, you must devote yourself to the process and be consistent in your exercises. You can gain an advantage over hitters by incorporating these workouts and advice into your program. Not only will you be in the best possible position to receive ground balls, but you will also be able to respond with lightning speed and transform yourself into a defensive force. This will leave the opposing teams feeling unhappy, putting your team one step closer to winning overall.

Strategies for handling

"Tough plays"

Shortstop is the most critical position on the defensive side of the infield, and you are the cornerstone of that position. Let's face it: not every ground ball is a routine play. This is a fact, but let's not pretend that it is. Occasionally, the ball will come crashing off the bat, make an unexpected hop, or force you to make an off-balance throw. These are all examples of situations that can occur. Is there any way you can make sure that you can handle these "tough plays" with poise and self-assurance? The following are some strategies that will assist you in becoming an expert in dealing with difficult circumstances:

Be Aware of and Prepare to Take on the Challenge

First and foremost, one must undergo a mindset shift to make progress. You shouldn't be afraid of challenging plays; instead, you should look at them as opportunities to show off your skills and improve your performance. Acknowledge the difficulty of the task at hand and have confidence in both your training and your instincts.

Quickly assess the current situation.

It just takes a fraction of a second to make significant decisions. Investigate the speed of the ball in addition to considering its path. Does it have a slow roller with a terrible hop, or does it have a line drive that is screaming? This will serve as the deciding factor in the approach that you select. Do you have any runners currently on base? You can establish the priority of your throwing if you are aware of the baserunner scenario. For instance, you can determine whether you should prioritize getting out first or throwing home. Are you slightly out of place regarding the position you play in the field? Your footwork needs to be adjusted rapidly while you keep your balance to reach the ball.

The fielding of the ball should be given the utmost responsibility.

To make the play, the first step is to catch the ball cleanly. When doing backhand plays, you should take a crossover step with the foot opposite the one you are using. This will allow you to move your body into a comfortable posture. Your ability to execute clean grounders on your backhand side will be enhanced. Maintain a low glove position and focus on securing the ball throughout the entire process of catching it. In the case of deep grounders, the highest attention should be placed on catching the ball first. To make a throw, you should control your momentum before performing. Accepting an exchange for something else is feasible when a flawless throw is made. It is conceivable that if you accidentally lose your balance, you shouldn't freak out. You should utilize your glove to catch the ball, even if it requires you to take a body position that is not typical.

Making Sure the Ball Is in the Right Place

Once you gain possession of the ball, you should prioritize making an accurate throw over a powerful one. If you want to cut down on wasted time, you should make a transfer from your glove to your throwing hand that is both quick and effective. The significance of this cannot be overstated when it comes to double plays. When it comes to throwing, proper footwork is essential to performing a robust and accurate throw. Maintaining a smooth pivot and generating power through the use of your lower body is also very crucial. The delivery of the ball to a specific place, such as the chest of the first baseman, is an essential aspect of the game that requires total concentration. It is crucial to avoid throwing with a lot of force because doing so will increase the likelihood of making mistakes.

Conversations with the Individuals Who Make Up Your Team

It is referred to as "Signal Plays." When conducting challenging double plays with runners on base, you must communicate your intentions to your teammate with hand signals that have been predetermined in advance. As an illustration, you may throw the ball home first. If you can make the play cleanly, you should not be afraid to ask for assistance from your second. You should not be scared to do so. If you do this, it is possible to avoid making mistakes to ensure the exit is successful.

Take notes on every play that you watch.

Play is always an opportunity to learn, regardless of whether it is a good or challenging activity. After a complex play, analyze what occurred to determine what went wrong. You didn't get the ball's direction in the appropriate direction, did you? Your footwork was terrible, didn't you think? Identify areas that could require some improvement and work on improving those aspects. During your practice sessions, you should use drills that simulate challenging situations that you have created. The ability to field grounders accurately, make throws while sprinting, and deal with circumstances in which they should be practiced. I ask that you maintain a close eye on the Masters: Pay attention to professional shortstops who are well-known for their exceptional defensive ability and how they respond to challenging situations, and then incorporate the strategies they employ into your game.

All shortstops will face difficult plays at some point in their careers; nevertheless, overcoming these challenges sets them apart from great shortstops. By maintaining a positive mindset, making it a point to grasp the ball cleanly, making precise throws, successfully interacting with others, and always learning new things, you have the potential to transform yourself into a self-assured and adaptable defender. You can efficiently perform even the most challenging plays if you are well-prepared and committed to achieving success and putting your defensive abilities to the test by going out into the world, accepting the challenge, and displaying your superiority!

CHAPTER 4

THE MENTAL GAME

Staying focused

"Through nine innings"

Baseball is not a race; instead, it is a challenge. In situations where the game lasts for an extended period, the score is close, or your side is having difficulty, nine innings can feel like a lifetime. To maximize your performance, it is essential to maintain your concentration throughout the entirety of the game. This is true regardless of whether you are a pitcher throwing heat in the first inning or a fielder making an essential play in the ninth. From the first pitch to the last out, here is a method to help you keep your laser concentration and remain sharp throughout the game.

The Importance of Maintaining Focus

Focusing intensely on the field is not the only way to achieve mental focus. All essential components are being present, actively participating in every play, and looking forward to what might occur next. When your mind is concentrated, you can respond more quickly to ground balls, anticipate pitches, and make decisions on defense. Concentration helps you maintain self-discipline and avoid mental blunders, which can result in errors that have significant financial consequences. Keeping your concentration for the entirety of the game enables you to consistently perform at your highest level, regardless of the circumstances.

The Obstacles and Difficulties in Maintaining Focus

Maintaining concentration for nine innings is a challenging task. As the game goes on, weariness may begin to set in, making it more difficult to maintain mental acuity throughout the game. Some external distractions might divert your attention away from the game. These include crowds, noises, and even your teammates. It is possible to experience irritation and doubt due to errors, poor calls, or a slump. This can make it difficult for you to concentrate on the task.

Techniques for achieving a more accurate focus

Establishing pre-game rituals that assist you in calming your mind and entering a state of concentration is a crucial step before a game. Activities such as deep breathing techniques, visualization exercises, or listening to calming music could fall under this category. Encourage yourself to replace negative ideas with positive affirmations by engaging in positive self-talk. Visualize yourself succeeding and remind yourself of the abilities you possess. Don't worry about the future or concentrate on mistakes you've made in the past; instead, stay in the here and now. Your primary focus should be your pitch, the current play, and the work. Ensure excellent posture and make eye contact with your coach or teammates. This is an essential part of body language. This tells your brain that you are actively engaged and concentrated on the task. Reduce the number of distractions that come from the outside. Shut off the sounds of the audience, pay no attention to conversations that aren't relevant, and concentrate exclusively on the game.

Maintaining Concentration Throughout the Entire Activity

Keeping yourself hydrated is essential since dehydration can cause weariness and reduce focus. Drink a lot of water throughout the game to keep your mind alert. Snacks that are good for you, such as fruits or nuts, can give you a quick burst of energy and help you fight fatigue, which can sometimes interfere with your ability to concentrate. During dead balls, it is essential to maintain engagement. In between pitches or innings, you should avoid zone out. Discuss strategies with your colleagues to keep your activity level, visualize upcoming plays, or stretch lightly. You must divide the game into more digestible parts to accomplish your short-term objectives. Concentrating on making a fantastic throw, securing an out, or hitting a clean line drive shot is essential. Reward yourself for maintaining your concentration and making successful plays. This is an example of positive reinforcement. This mental congratulation has the potential to reward conduct that is positive.

Mental Toughness

A mental game is just as important as a physical game in baseball. Allow yourself to let go of mistakes to overcome frustration rapidly. You should not dwell on a poor play; instead, you should focus on the next opportunity. If you are under pressure, you should maintain your composure. Take a few deep breaths and have a positive attitude. Embrace the Challenge: View difficult circumstances as opportunities to demonstrate your ability to concentrate and your mental fortitude.

Practice and self-control are required to keep one's concentration for nine innings. Suppose you implement these tactics and work on strengthening your mental toughness. In that case, you can convert yourself from an easily distracted player into an athlete who can flourish under pressure and maintain a laser-like focus. Throughout the game, you will be present for every play, able to make intelligent decisions and perform to the best of your abilities. Step onto the field with an uncluttered mindset and a concentrated spirit

---

Handling errors

"And bouncing back."

It is a game of inches and judgments made in a split second in baseball. The most skilled players are nevertheless prone to making mistakes. Your frustration, loss, and possibly even the feeling of hanging your head in shame can be brought on by a misjudged fly ball, a bobbled grounder, or a wayward throw. Dwelling on mistakes, on the other hand, is a prescription for disaster. One of the most reliable indicators of a great player is their capacity to recover quickly and with self-assurance after a setback. The following is a handbook that will assist you in transforming obstacles into steppingstones, gaining knowledge from your blunders, and emerging from mistakes more potent than ever before.

Errors provide an emotional roller coaster.

Making mistakes is not a fun job. You may experience feelings of frustration with yourself, including doubts about your capabilities and skills. The pressure to perform flawlessly can lead to feelings of guilt, mainly if your misstep causes your team to lose runs or momentum. You may feel angry with yourself, the scenario, or your teammates. You may also feel upset about the situation.

Putting an end to the vicious cycle of negativity

Maintaining a fixation on these feelings is counterproductive. Do not attempt to ignore the mistake; acknowledge it briefly, but don't let it consume your thoughts. You are responsible for your error; apologize to your coach and teammates, but try to avoid feeling sorry for yourself. Encourage yourself to replace negative ideas with positive affirmations by engaging in positive self-talk. Bring your skills and accomplishments from the past to your attention.

It is essential to learn from your mistakes.

Learning experiences can be gained from making mistakes. Think about what went wrong and assess the situation. Are you erroneously judging the ball? You had a horrible footwork, didn't you? Find out what the cause is. Have a conversation with your coach or a trusted team member to receive constructive criticism and direction on how to avoid making errors of a similar nature in the future. Picture yourself successfully carrying out the play that you made a mistake on. You may boost your confidence and performance by engaging in mental rehearsal.

In the spirit of moving forward with confidence

The short-term focus is to ensure you do not allow the blunder to remain in your mind. Pay attention to the next move and the chance to make up for your actions. Even though you made a mistake, you should have faith in your skills and the instruction you have received. If you lacked confidence in your abilities, you would not be on the field. Positive body language includes maintaining a tall posture, maintaining eye contact with your teammates, and projecting an air of self-assurance. Increasing your morale and motivating your colleagues by maintaining a pleasant disposition is possible.

Developing Mental Toughness

View errors as opportunities to learn and grow, not setbacks that define you. Focus on the things you can control – your effort, attitude, and execution on the next play. Observe how professional players handle errors. They accept responsibility, move on, and focus on the next play.

Everyone is capable of making errors. The best players use them as fuel to better their game. For example, suppose you are a player easily discouraged by mistakes. In that case, you may become a resilient athlete who thrives under pressure by cultivating a positive mindset, welcoming learning chances, and bouncing back confidently. Now is the time to pick yourself up, take a few deep breaths, and prepare to dominate the forthcoming match! Have faith in yourself!

Leading the infield

"And being a vocal presence."

Being an infielder means that you are accountable not only for your position but also for being the quarterback of the infield, the leader on the field who is in charge of orchestrating the defensive symphony. Leadership is not simply a matter of issuing instructions; it is achieved through effective communication, proactive positioning, and the ability to inspire teammates through verbal and physical actions. The following is a course of action that will help you become a genuine infield leader who commands respect and improves the defensive performance of your squad.

The Influence of Communication on the World

To guarantee that everyone is in the appropriate places and aware of the defensive play being called, it is essential to do pre-pitch alignment before each pitch. Situational awareness requires you to alert your teammates to baserunner scenarios, such as the number of outs or the possibility of stolen bases, so they know the situation. It is essential to make it clear that fly balls or line drives are being called out to prevent collisions and ensure that everyone knows who is taking the catch.

"Words Are Important "

Use language that is positive and encouraging. Use language that is positive and encouraging. Encourage your teammates after making a good play and avoid negativity after making a mistake. Please ensure that your communication is both clear and concise. Never yell or use jargon that is difficult to understand. It is important to note that being forceful is not the same as being bossy. Instead of making demands, set an example by offering constructive suggestions.

Taking the initiative to lead

Demonstrate the significance of hustle to your teammates by consistently playing with one hundred percent effort, even in routine plays. Ensure that your body language conveys an air of conviction. Maintain an upright posture, look the person in the eye, and exude an air of command. The ability to anticipate plays and events is referred to as situational awareness. You should adjust your position proactively depending on the batter, the number of pitches, or the number of baserunners.

Acquiring Respect: An Example

Set an example for others to follow by becoming the most diligent worker on the field. You should be the first person to arrive for practice and the last person to go. Knowledge is power. Therefore, you should study the game, learn the various defensive techniques, and be a resource for your teammates. If you want to be approachable, you should create an atmosphere where your co-workers are comfortable asking questions or seeking guidance.

Establishing Yourself as a Vocal Leader

Certain people are not born with the ability to be vocal leaders. To begin, you should start by communicating well in straightforward settings. As your self-assurance rises, gradually increase the amount of verbal presence you have. Pay attention to how other leaders in the field communicate and integrate strategies you discovered successfully. Engage in role-playing defensive scenarios with your teammates, during which you will focus on improving your leadership and communication skills.

The Process of Creating a Cohesive Unit

Establishing positive relationships with your infielders on and off the field is an essential part of developing team chemistry—the presence of trust and camaraderie results in improved communication and collaboration among team members. Hold yourselves and your teammates accountable for mistakes but do it in a constructive manner and in private so you can keep the atmosphere sound. Celebrate together the victories that the defense team has achieved. This helps to improve morale among the team and reinforces good plays.

A journey, not a destination, is what leadership is all about. You can turn yourself from a passive infielder into the outspoken leader your team requires if you commit to clear communication, proactive actions, and encouraging your colleagues. In orchestrating a defensive masterpiece, you will garner respect, raise team spirit, and leave opposing hitters feeling discouraged. Now is the time to take leadership, be the leader your squad will need, and dominate the infield!

CHAPTER 5

PRE-GAME AND TRAINING

Effective practice routines

The sport of baseball is a game that requires ability, strategy, and consistent practice. But if you only have limited time to practice, how can you ensure you get the most out of your development? The answer is to develop efficient practice routines that focus on specific areas of weakness, improve abilities applicable in a variety of contexts, and manage to keep things interesting. The following is a program that will assist you in changing your practice sessions from meaningless drills into concentrated workouts that will propel you toward becoming a baseball expert.

What is the significance of planning

You shouldn't just attend practice and take a chance on the outcome. You should know your goals and identify areas you may develop, such as hitting, fielding, and throwing. Ensure your practice program is tailored to address those areas of weakness. Avoid becoming mired down in a rut! Keeping things exciting and focusing on different parts of your game can be accomplished by incorporating a range of drills and exercises into your routine. Your practice should be organized with a defined timetable, and you should set up time for each key talent, which ensures that you do not overlook any essential aspects.

Utilizing Your Time to Its Fullest Potential

It is important to always begin with a dynamic warm-up to prepare your body for strenuous exercise and prevent injuries. Additionally, it is important to prioritize quality over quantity when it comes to your workouts. Keep your attention on the correct technique and execution throughout each practice. Put yourself to the test by performing just a little bit beyond. This is how you will make progress.

Practice is the only way to make progress, not perfection.

Errors are unavoidable, but they also present chances for great learning. Examine your mistakes and make use of them to learn and grow. Set goals that are attainable and monitor your progress to maintain your motivation. You may keep your motivation along the journey by celebrating even the smallest of your successes. Practice does not have to be a burdensome activity. To maintain interest in the activity, include some exciting exercises and challenges.

Beyond the Scope of Solo Work

Practice with your fellow players. Perform simulated game scenarios, focus on improving your communication skills, and encourage others to improve. Do not hesitate to approach instructors or experienced players for feedback and help with your practice routines. This is an important step that you should not be scared to take. Pay attention to the professional players as they train or watch videos that provide coaching. You should take the time to learn from their methods and then adopt them into your routine.

Effective practice regimens are not universally applicable to all situations. Experiment, figure out what works best for you, and adjust your strategy consistently. Your practice sessions will become the cornerstone of your baseball development if you are dedicated, wise in planning, and have a positive outlook. They will make you a well-rounded player ready to dominate on the field.

Strength and conditioning

"For shortstops"

You're the defensive anchor and athletic master of the infield as a shortstop. To catch rockets, turn double plays, and throw hard, you need to be quick, strong, and able to move quickly. But these skills don't just appear; they're built with a specific strength and conditioning routine. To become a famous shortstop, here's how to strengthen your body.

Core Strength is King

Your core is the engine that sends energy to every part of your body. Get powerful enough to throw like a laser across the diamond. Stability: Stay balanced during dives, jumps, and quick direction changes. Injury Prevention: A strong core helps protect your back from the stresses of throwing and fielding.

What You Need to Do to Get a Champion Core

Do side, high, and medicine ball planks to work your core. Russian Twists: Rotate your torso while holding a weight to work your obliques. Anti-Rotational Exercises: These exercises strengthen your core's ability to resist rotation, which is essential for staying stable during throws.

Getting Stronger Legs

Do squats and lunges properly to get the most out of them and build leg strength. Plyometric workouts, such as box jumps and jump squats, help you build explosive power. These allow you to jump higher, change directions faster, and make those fantastic flying catches that will stop your heart.

Do not forget about the upper body.

Do push-ups and pull-ups to strengthen your upper body. These exercises work your chest, shoulders, and back, which helps with how you throw and handle the bat. Exercise with a medicine ball to improve your upper body balance and rotational strength.

Being steady is essential. Aim for two to three weekly strength training sessions, ensuring you have time to heal. Pay attention to your body, focus on good form over heavy weights, and get personalized advice from a teacher or trainer. By strategically building your strength and fitness, you'll become a shortstop who commands respect on the field and confuses your opponents with how good you are at defense.

Scouting reports

"And game preparation"

When it comes to sports, knowledge is power. For better or worse, knowing your opponent before you play can make a difference. The best way to get ahead is to use scouting reports and plan your game strategically:

Scouting reports are your secret weapon.

You can learn a lot about your opponent from scouting reports. These reports, which leaders or scouts make, list the good and bad points of the other team, especially their batters. Figure out how a player hits the ball. Does he swing early in the count? Does he pull the ball a lot? You can make more effective pitches if you know about these habits. Does the batter have trouble with fastballs or breaking pitches? This information can be found in scouting reports, which can help you write a good pitching sequence. Does the other team have a history of stealing bases? Knowing how they usually run the bases helps your team prepare for possible stolen base tries.

Putting what you know to use

You can't use the information in scouting reports if you don't use it. Use the scouting report to help you and your teachers create a game plan. This could mean using different defense shifts or certain pitches against certain batters. "Internalize the Information" means reading the scouting report before the game and picturing yourself following the plan. You can use the information better if you are already familiar with it. Tell your friends, especially your catcher, what you've learned. Open conversation ensures everyone is on the same page when you play the other team.

Not Just Scout Reports

If you can, watch the other team's game film. This can give you a visual confirmation of the details in the scouting report and help you understand their general strategy. Know what the weather will be like on game day and how the direction and strength of the wind can change the ball's movement. Figuring out the field's size and surface can help you choose a pitch and set up your defense.

Making scouting reports and getting ready for games is an ongoing process. As the game progresses and you learn more, you should change your approach to reflect that. You can go from being a quiet player to a strategic force on the field, ready to take advantage of weaknesses and beat the other teams if you use scouting reports well and are always prepared for anything.

CLOSING THOUGHTS

Excellent work! You've made it to the bottom of the ninth in your quest to become a Shortstop Supreme. You've worked hard to improve your fielding skills, turn your instincts into a sixth sense, and become mentally tough enough to command respect on the ground. Baseball, on the other hand, is a game that you can play for a lifetime. Take on the obstacles, learn something from every play, and try to improve.

Committing to focused practice sessions over and over again is a must. Muscle memory is built through repetition, which also makes sure that you can do well under pressure. Set up regular times to practice, and don't be afraid to try new drills to keep things interesting. Like life, baseball can be a wild ride. Make goals that you can reach and be proud of your growth. Also, learn from your mistakes. Don't forget that your love for the game is what drives you. When you lose inspiration, think about your goals again, picture yourself succeeding, and spark that drive that got you here in the first place. Be an example for your teammates by working hard, always being on the go, and having a good mood. A real boss makes everyone on the team better. Motivate your teammates by what you do on and off the field and make the setting supportive and positive. Baseball is a lovely game. Enjoy the friendships you make with your teammates, the thrill of competing against other people who push you to your limits, and the pure joy of making amazing plays. Keep your eye on the end goal and don't miss the trip along the way. Remember the friends you made, the lessons you learned, and the experiences you made along the way. As soon as you leave the field, take a deep breath and think about how much you've changed. You are no longer just a hopeful shortstop; you are now a formidable defender. Shortstop Supreme, the story doesn't end here! Keep going beyond your limits, be open to new challenges, and keep writing your own baseball history. Don't forget that the gem is waiting for your next brilliant move!

9 7 9 8 2 2 7 9 2 8 7 6 4